Babylon

Ancient Babylon was a really cool city that existed a long time ago in a place called Mesopotamia, which is now part of modern-day Iraq. It was around 2300 BCE when Babylon started, and it lasted for quite a while before it faded away.

What made Babylon special was where it

was located. It sat between two rivers, the Tigris and Euphrates, which made the land around it very fertile. This meant that Babylonians could grow lots of food, which helped the city grow and become prosperous. Plus, being near these rivers was handy for trade and transportation.

One of the most famous things about Babylon was the Tower of Babel, also known as the Etemenanki. This huge tower was like a giant pyramid, and it was built to honor the Babylonian god Marduk. It was so tall that you could see it from far away, and people were amazed by its size and beauty.

In Babylon, there were different groups of people, each with their own roles. At the top were the kings and priests, who were in charge of making rules and leading religious ceremonies. Then there were regular folks who worked as farmers, craftsmen, or traders. At the bottom were slaves who had to work hard without getting paid.

Religion was a big part of life in Babylon. The Babylonians believed in many gods and goddesses, and they built temples to worship them. The most important god was Marduk, who they thought protected their city. People would pray and offer sacrifices to these gods to keep them happy and get their blessings.

The Babylonians were pretty smart too. They had their own set of rules called laws, which everyone had to follow. The most famous set of laws was called the Code of Hammurabi, named after one of Babylon's kings. It had rules for things like stealing, fighting, and even building houses.

Trade was really important in Babylon. The city had busy markets where people bought and sold all kinds of things like food, clothes, and jewelry. Merchants from Babylon traveled to other lands to trade their goods, and they brought back stuff from faraway places too.

Babylon was also known for its amazing buildings. The Ishtar Gate, for example, was a beautiful entrance to the city, decorated with colorful bricks showing animals and gods. And then there were the Hanging Gardens of Babylon, which were like a paradise with plants growing on big terraces.

But Babylon wasn't always peaceful. At times, it faced attacks from other civilizations like the Assyrians. These wars caused a lot of damage to the city, but Babylonians were resilient and always managed to rebuild and make things better.

One of the greatest periods in Babylon's history was when King Nebuchadnezzar II ruled. He was a powerful king who built many grand structures and made Babylon even more magnificent. Under his rule, the city flourished and became a center of art, culture, and learning.

Sadly, Babylon's greatness didn't last forever. In 539 BCE, it was conquered by the Persian king Cyrus the Great. After that,

Babylon lost some of its importance and never fully recovered.

Over time, Babylon faded away, and its once-great buildings fell into ruins. Today, all that's left are the remnants of this ancient civilization, buried beneath the earth. But even though Babylon is gone, its legacy lives on, reminding us of the incredible achievements of this remarkable city.

Ancient Egypt

Ancient Egypt was an incredible civilization that existed a long, long time ago, thousands of years before today. It was a fascinating place with lots of amazing things to see and learn about.

Egypt was famous for being home to the mighty Nile River, which was like a lifeline for the people who lived there. Every year, when the Nile flooded, it left behind rich, fertile soil that was perfect for growing crops. This made Egypt a great place to live and helped the civilization thrive.

One of the most iconic symbols of ancient Egypt was the pyramids. These enormous structures were built as tombs for the pharaohs, who were the rulers of Egypt. The pyramids were made of huge blocks of stone and were incredibly tall. People from all over the world still marvel at their size and wonder how they were built.

The pharaohs were like kings, but they were also seen as gods by the ancient Egyptians. They ruled over the land and made important decisions about things like laws and wars. They were also responsible for overseeing the building of temples and monuments dedicated to the gods.

Religion played a huge role in ancient Egyptian life. The Egyptians believed in many gods and goddesses, each with their own special powers and responsibilities. They built magnificent temples to worship these gods and held elaborate ceremonies and festivals in their honor.

One of the most famous gods was Ra, the

sun god, who was believed to travel across the sky each day in a boat. Another important god was Osiris, the god of the afterlife, who judged the souls of the dead. The ancient Egyptians believed that if they lived a good life, they would be rewarded in the afterlife.

The ancient Egyptians were also known for their incredible art and architecture. They created beautiful statues, paintings, and jewelry that still amaze people today. They also built grand temples and palaces, many of which still stand as a testament to their skill and craftsmanship.

One of the most important inventions of ancient Egypt was hieroglyphics, which was their form of writing. Hieroglyphics were made up of pictures and symbols that represented different sounds and words. They were used to write down important information like laws, stories, and prayers.

Trade was also very important to the ancient Egyptians. They traded goods like gold, linen, and grain with other civilizations in the region. They even traded with people from faraway lands like

Greece and Mesopotamia.

Life in ancient Egypt wasn't always easy. The people had to work hard to grow their crops and build their monuments. They also had to deal with things like floods, diseases, and invasions from other civilizations.

But despite these challenges, the ancient

Egyptians were able to create a rich and vibrant civilization that has captured the imagination of people around the world. Their legacy lives on in the magnificent ruins and artifacts that still remain, giving us a glimpse into their fascinating world.

Greece

Ancient Greece was a magical place filled with stories of gods, heroes, and mighty warriors. It existed a long time ago, thousands of years before our time, but its legacy still lives on today in books, movies, and even the Olympic Games.

Greece was made up of many city-states, each with its own government and way of life. The most famous of these city-states were Athens and Sparta. Athens was known for its democracy, where people could vote on important decisions, while Sparta was known for its fierce warriors and strict way of life.

One of the things that made ancient Greece so special was its mythology. The Greeks believed in a pantheon of gods and goddesses who lived on Mount Olympus, the highest mountain in Greece. These gods and goddesses were like superhumans with special powers, and they were always getting up to mischief.

Some of the most famous gods and goddesses were Zeus, the king of the gods; Athena, the goddess of wisdom; and Poseidon, the god of the sea. There were also lots of stories about heroes like Hercules, who performed amazing feats of strength, and Perseus, who fought terrifying monsters.

The ancient Greeks loved to tell stories, and many of these stories were passed down through generations. They believed that by telling these stories, they could learn important lessons about life, courage, and honor.

Another thing that ancient Greece was

famous for was its art and architecture. The Greeks built magnificent temples, theaters, and statues that still amaze people today. They were especially skilled at making pottery, which they decorated with intricate designs and scenes from their mythology.

One of the most famous buildings in ancient Greece was the Parthenon, a temple dedicated to the goddess Athena. It was built in Athens and is considered one of the greatest achievements of ancient Greek architecture.

The ancient Greeks were also great thinkers and philosophers. They asked questions about the world around them and tried to understand the meaning of life. Some of the most famous Greek philosophers were Socrates, Plato, and

Aristotle, who taught their students about subjects like ethics, politics, and the nature of reality.

Education was very important in ancient Greece, especially in Athens. Boys went to school to learn reading, writing, and arithmetic, as well as subjects like music, art, and athletics.

Girls were taught at home by their mothers and learned skills like weaving and cooking.

The ancient Greeks were also skilled athletes and held athletic competitions called the Olympic Games. These games were held every four years in the city of Olympia and included events like running, wrestling, and chariot racing. The winners of these games were considered heroes and were celebrated throughout Greece.

Life in ancient Greece wasn't always easy. The Greeks had to deal with wars, natural disasters, and diseases, just like people do today. But they were also able to create a rich and vibrant civilization that has had a lasting impact on the world.

Today, we can still see the influence of ancient

Greece all around us. We study their myths and legends, admire their art and architecture, and even compete in their Olympic Games. The legacy of ancient Greece reminds us of the power of human creativity and the enduring quest for knowledge and understanding.

Persia

Ancient Persia was a fascinating civilization that thrived in the region we now call Iran. It existed a long time ago, thousands of years before our time, but its legacy still echoes through history books and stories told by people around the world.

One of the most famous things about ancient Persia was its mighty kings, known as the Persian emperors. These emperors ruled over a vast empire that stretched across many lands, from Egypt in the west to India in the east.

They were powerful rulers who commanded huge armies and built magnificent palaces and cities.

One of the most famous Persian emperors was Cyrus the Great, who founded the Persian Empire around 550 BCE. He was known for his wisdom and kindness, and he treated the people he conquered with respect and fairness. Under his rule, the Persian Empire grew to become one of the largest and most powerful in the world.

Another famous Persian emperor was Darius the Great, who came after Cyrus. He was known for his administrative skills and for building the first postal system in the world, called the Royal Road. This road stretched for thousands of miles and allowed messages and travelers to move quickly across the empire.

The Persians were also known for their religion, which was called Zoroastrianism. This religion was founded by the prophet Zoroaster and taught that there were two forces in the world: good and evil. People who followed Zoroastrianism believed in being kind, truthful, and honest, and they worshipped in temples called fire temples.

One of the most famous buildings in ancient Persia was the city of Persepolis, which was built by Darius the Great. It was a magnificent city with huge palaces, temples, and statues, all decorated with intricate carvings and colorful paintings. Persepolis was the center of Persian power and culture for many years.

The Persians were also known for their art and architecture. They created beautiful pottery, jewelry, and textiles, as well as grand buildings and monuments. One of the most famous examples of Persian art is the Cyrus Cylinder, a clay cylinder inscribed with the words of Cyrus the Great, which is considered one of the first human rights documents in history.

The ancient Persians were also great engineers and builders. They built huge irrigation systems to bring water to their fields and cities, as well as impressive roads and bridges to connect their empire.

They were also skilled at making weapons and armor, which helped them conquer new lands and defend their empire from enemies.

Trade was also very important to the ancient Persians. They traded goods like silk, spices, and precious metals with other civilizations in the region, as well as with people from faraway lands like China and Greece. They also built a network of roads and ports to make it easier to trade with other countries.

Life in ancient Persia wasn't always easy. The Persians had to deal with wars, invasions, and natural disasters, just like people do today. But they were also able to create a rich and diverse civilization that has left a lasting impact on the world.

Today, we can still see the influence of ancient Persia in many aspects of our lives. We study their history and culture, admire their art and architecture, and even use some of their inventions and ideas in our own lives. The legacy of ancient Persia reminds us of the power of human ingenuity and the importance of understanding and

appreciating other cultures.

Rome

Ancient Rome was an incredible civilization that existed a long time ago, thousands of years before our time. It was a mighty empire that stretched across much of Europe, Africa, and

Asia, leaving a lasting impact on the world.

One of the most famous things about ancient Rome was its legendary city, Rome itself. Rome started as a small village on the banks of the Tiber River and grew into one of the largest and most powerful cities in the ancient world. It was the heart of the Roman

Empire and the center of Roman culture, politics, and power.

The Romans were known for their

incredible buildings and engineering feats. They built magnificent structures like the Colosseum, a huge arena where gladiators fought to entertain the crowds, and the Pantheon, a temple dedicated to the gods with a massive dome roof. They also built impressive roads, bridges, and aqueducts that helped connect their empire and bring water to their cities.

Another famous thing about ancient Rome was its system of government. The Romans had a republic, which meant that the people could vote for their leaders. They had a Senate, which was a group of wealthy and powerful men who made the laws and decisions for the city. They also had consuls, who were like presidents, and magistrates, who were like judges.

The Romans were also famous for their

military might. They had a huge army made up of well-trained soldiers who were experts at fighting on land and at sea. They conquered many lands and defeated many enemies, including the Carthaginians, Greeks, and Gauls. Their soldiers were disciplined and brave, and they fought with spears, swords, and shields.

One of the most famous Roman leaders was Julius Caesar, who was a great general and politician. He conquered Gaul (which is now France) and made himself dictator of Rome. He was loved by the people but hated by the Senate, and he was eventually assassinated by a group of senators who feared his power.

After Julius Caesar's death, Rome fell into chaos, but eventually, a new emperor rose to power: Augustus. He was Julius Caesar's nephew and adopted son, and he became the first emperor of Rome. He ruled for over 40 years and brought peace and stability to the empire, which became known as the Pax Romana, or Roman Peace.

During the Pax Romana, Rome flourished. It was a time of great prosperity and progress, with advances in art, literature, and science. The Romans built grand buildings, wrote epic poems, and made important discoveries in fields like medicine and engineering.

But life in ancient Rome wasn't always easy. The empire faced many challenges, including invasions by barbarian tribes, political corruption, and economic instability. There were also many social problems, like slavery and poverty, and the gap between the rich and the poor grew wider over time.

Despite these challenges, Rome continued to thrive for many centuries. It was a beacon of civilization and culture in a world filled with darkness and chaos. But eventually, the empire began to decline, and in 476 AD, it fell to barbarian invaders, bringing an end to the ancient Roman Empire.

Today, we can still see the influence of ancient Rome all around us. We study their history and culture, admire their art and architecture, and even use their language and legal systems in our own lives. The legacy of ancient Rome reminds us of the power of human achievement and the importance of learning from the past.

Maya

Ancient Maya was a fascinating civilization that thrived in the lush jungles of Central America, in what is now Mexico, Guatemala, Belize, Honduras, and El Salvador. Even though it existed a long time ago, thousands of years before our time, its legacy still captures our imagination today.

The Maya civilization was made up of many city-states, each with its own ruler and government. These city-states were connected by trade and shared culture, but they were also independent and sometimes fought with each other.

One of the most famous things about the ancient Maya was their incredible cities and temples. They built huge pyramids, palaces, and ball courts out of stone, which still stand today as a testament to their skill and craftsmanship. These cities were centers of culture and religion, where priests performed ceremonies and rulers held court.

The Maya were also known for their advanced knowledge of astronomy and mathematics. They studied the movements of the stars and planets and created accurate calendars to track time. They also invented a system of writing using hieroglyphs, which they carved into stone and wrote on bark paper.

Religion played a central role in ancient Maya life. They believed in many gods and goddesses, who controlled the forces of nature and the cycles of life. They built temples and made offerings to these gods to ask for their blessings and protection.

One of the most important gods in the

Maya pantheon was Kukulkan, the feathered serpent god. He was believed to bring rain and fertility to the land and was worshipped in temples called pyramids.

The most famous of these pyramids is El Castillo, which is located at the ancient city of Chichen Itza in Mexico.

Another important aspect of ancient Maya culture was their ball game, which they played in huge ball courts. The game was a ritual and had religious significance, with players wearing elaborate costumes and using their hips to hit a rubber ball through stone hoops. The winners were honored as heroes, while the losers sometimes faced a gruesome fate.

Life in ancient Maya wasn't always easy. The Maya faced many challenges, including wars, droughts, and diseases. But they were also able to create a rich and vibrant civilization that has left a lasting impact on the world.

The ancient Maya civilization reached its peak during the Classic Period, from about 250 to 900 AD. During this time, the Maya built many of their most famous cities and temples and made important advances in art, science, and culture.

But around 900 AD, something mysterious

happened, and many of the great Maya cities were abandoned. Scholars aren't sure exactly why this happened, but it may have been due to a combination of factors, including overpopulation, environmental degradation, and warfare.

After the collapse of their civilization, the Maya continued to live in the region, but their cities were gradually reclaimed by the jungle, and their culture and traditions began to fade away. It wasn't until the 19th century that scholars began to rediscover the ancient Maya civilization and unlock its secrets.

Today, we can still see the influence of ancient Maya in many aspects of our lives. We study their history and culture, admire their art and architecture, and even use their calendar in our daily lives. The legacy of the ancient Maya reminds us of the power of human creativity and the importance of preserving our past.

The Aztecs

The ancient Aztecs were an incredible civilization that lived in what is now Mexico, thousands of years ago. They were a powerful and advanced society, known for their mighty warriors, intricate artwork, and complex religious beliefs.

The Aztec civilization was made up of many city-states, the most famous of which was Tenochtitlan. This city was built on an island in the middle of Lake Texcoco and was the capital of the Aztec Empire. It was a huge and bustling city, with grand palaces, temples, and marketplaces.

One of the most famous things about the Aztecs was their incredible pyramids and temples. They built huge stone structures, like the Templo Mayor, which was dedicated to their main god, Huitzilopochtli. This temple was the center of religious life in

Tenochtitlan, where priests performed ceremonies and made offerings to the gods.

The Aztecs were also known for their

incredible artwork. They created beautiful pottery, jewelry, and textiles, often decorated with intricate designs and bright colors. They also carved elaborate sculptures and made intricate paintings on walls and codices, which were books made from bark paper.

Religion played a central role in Aztec life. They believed in many gods and goddesses, who controlled the forces of nature and the cycles of life. They made offerings to these gods to ask for their blessings and protection, often sacrificing animals or even humans in elaborate ceremonies.

One of the most important gods in the Aztec pantheon was Quetzalcoatl, the feathered serpent god. He was believed to bring knowledge and wisdom to the people and was worshipped in temples across the empire. Another important god was Tlaloc, the rain god, who was believed to bring water to the crops and protect the people from drought.

The Aztecs were also skilled warriors and built a powerful army. They conquered many lands and defeated many enemies, using weapons like spears, clubs, and bows and arrows. They also wore armor made from animal skins and used shields to protect themselves in battle.

Life in ancient Aztec wasn't always easy. The Aztecs faced many challenges, including wars, droughts, and diseases. But they were also able to create a rich and vibrant civilization that has left a lasting impact on the world.

The Aztec civilization reached its peak during the 15th and early 16th centuries, just before the arrival of the Spanish conquistadors. But in 1521, the Spanish conquistador Hernan Cortes conquered Tenochtitlan and brought an end to the Aztec Empire. The Aztec civilization was devastated by disease, warfare, and forced labor, and much of their culture and traditions were lost.

Today, we can still see the influence of ancient Aztec in many aspects of our lives. We study their history and culture, admire their artwork and architecture, and even use some of their words and foods in our daily lives. The legacy of the ancient Aztec reminds us of the power of human creativity and the importance of preserving our past.

China

Ancient China was a remarkable civilization that flourished in East Asia, thousands of years ago. It was a land of emperors, scholars, warriors, and artisans, known for its rich culture, advanced technology, and enduring traditions.

China was ruled by many different dynasties over thousands of years, each with its own emperors and rulers. These dynasties included the Shang, Zhou, Qin, Han, Tang, Song, and Ming, among others. Each dynasty left its mark on Chinese history, contributing to the country's cultural, political, and economic development.

One of the most famous things about ancient China was its inventions and technological innovations. The ancient Chinese invented many things that are still used today, such as paper, printing, gunpowder, and the compass. They also built the Great Wall of China, a massive defensive structure that stretches for thousands of miles across northern China.

Another important aspect of ancient Chinese civilization was its philosophy and religion. The ancient Chinese believed in many gods and spirits, and they practiced rituals and ceremonies to honor them. They also followed different philosophical traditions, such as Confucianism,

Daoism, and Buddhism, which taught moral values, harmony with nature, and the pursuit of enlightenment.

The ancient Chinese were also known for their incredible artwork and architecture. They created beautiful pottery, paintings, and sculptures, often decorated with intricate designs and colorful patterns. They also built grand palaces, temples, and gardens, which were designed to harmonize with the natural world.

One of the most famous buildings in ancient China was the Forbidden City, which was the imperial palace of the Ming and Qing dynasties. It was a massive complex of buildings, gardens, and courtyards, surrounded by high walls and guarded by soldiers. Only the emperor and his family were allowed to enter the Forbidden

City, making it a symbol of imperial power and authority.

The ancient Chinese were also skilled writers and scholars. They wrote many books and texts on subjects like history, literature, philosophy, and science. Some of the most famous works include the Analects of Confucius, the Dao De

Jing, and the Art of War by Sun Tzu.

Life in ancient China wasn't always easy. The Chinese faced many challenges, including wars, famines, and natural disasters. But they were also able to create a rich and vibrant civilization that has left a lasting impact on the world.

The ancient Chinese civilization reached its peak during the Han dynasty, from about 206 BCE to 220 CE. During this time, China experienced a period of great prosperity and stability, with advances in art, science, and culture. The Han dynasty also expanded China's borders, making it one of the largest empires in the world.

But the glory of the Han dynasty eventually faded, and China entered a period of turmoil and chaos known as the Three Kingdoms period. This was followed by centuries of division and conflict, as different dynasties rose and fell, each struggling to unite the country under their rule.

In 221 BCE, China was finally reunited under the rule of the Qin dynasty, which introduced many reforms and innovations. The Qin dynasty also built the first version of the Great Wall of China, which was later expanded and rebuilt by subsequent dynasties.

Today, we can still see the influence of ancient China in many aspects of our lives. We study their history and culture, admire their art and architecture, and use their inventions and ideas in our daily lives. The legacy of ancient China reminds us of the power of human creativity and the importance of preserving our past.

The Minoans

Ancient Crete was a fascinating civilization that thrived on the island of Crete, located in the Mediterranean Sea, thousands of years ago. It was a land of myths, legends, and extraordinary achievements, known for its advanced culture, majestic palaces, and intricate artwork.

The ancient Cretans were known as the Minoans, named after their legendary king, King Minos. They lived during the Bronze Age, around 3000 to 1100 BCE, making them one of the earliest advanced civilizations in Europe.

One of the most remarkable things about ancient Crete was its magnificent palaces. The most famous of these palaces was the Palace of Knossos, located near the modern-day city of Heraklion. The Palace of Knossos was a vast complex of buildings, with grand halls, luxurious rooms, and colorful frescoes decorating the walls. It was the center of Minoan civilization, where the king and his court lived and ruled over the island.

The Minoans were also skilled artists and craftsmen. They created beautiful pottery, jewelry, and sculptures, often decorated with intricate designs and vibrant colors. They also made elaborate frescoes, which were paintings done on wet plaster, depicting scenes from everyday life, mythology, and religious ceremonies.

Religion played an important role in Minoan society. The Minoans worshipped many gods and goddesses, including the Mother Goddess, who was believed to be the source of all life, and the Bull God, who was associated with fertility and power. They held religious ceremonies and festivals to honor these gods and ask for their blessings.

One of the most famous legends of

ancient Crete was the story of the Minotaur. According to legend, King Minos had a labyrinth built beneath the Palace of Knossos to imprison the Minotaur, a fearsome creature with the body of a man and the head of a bull. Every year, seven young men and seven young women from Athens were sent as tribute to be sacrificed to the Minotaur, until the hero Theseus arrived and defeated the creature.

Life in ancient Crete wasn't always easy. The Minoans faced many challenges, including earthquakes, volcanic eruptions, and invasions from other civilizations. But they were also able to create a rich and prosperous society that flourished for many centuries.

The decline of the Minoan civilization is still a mystery to historians and archaeologists. Some believe that it was caused by a catastrophic event, such as a volcanic eruption or an invasion by the Mycenaeans, another ancient civilization from mainland Greece. Others think that it may have been due to social unrest or economic decline.

Despite the decline of the Minoan civilization, its legacy lives on today. The Palace of Knossos and other archaeological sites on the island of Crete continue to attract visitors from around the world, who come to marvel at the achievements of this ancient civilization. The Minoans may be gone, but their memory lives on in the myths, legends, and artifacts that they left behind.

Made in the USA
Coppell, TX
29 March 2024

30686709R10075